Y0-BDC-534

BAD NAMES FOR WOMEN

BAD NAMES FOR WOMEN

HILARY THAM

WORD WORKS CAPITAL COLLECTION

Bad Names for Women
Copyright © 1989 by Hilary Tham
Printed in the U.S.A.

First Edition   First Printing

Reproduction of any part of this book in any form or by any means,
electronic or mechanical, including photocopying, recording or by any
information storage and retrieval system must be with permission in
writing from the publisher. Address inquiries to: The Word Works, PO
Box 42164, Washington, DC 20015.

Typography by Kathryn E. King
Cover by Robert J. Groner
Graphic design by Janice Olson

Library of Congress Catalog Card Number: 89-050242
International Standard Book Number: 0-915380-23-4

Some of the poems in this collection have appeared in an earlier version
in the following publications to whose editors grateful acknowledgment
is made: *Antietam Review*—"Dayenu," "Breach," "Lint Filter"; *Delhi-
London Poetry Quarterly*—"Mountains," "Eve," "The Naming"; *Gar-
goyle*—"May Means Beautiful in Chinese"; *Irene Leach Literary Contest
1988 Winners Anthology*—"Daughter of Survivors" ("Second Genera-
tion Jew"); *Lip Service*—"Kitefighting Season," "Elaine"; *Pig Iron*—
"Mrs. Wei in America"; *Wind*—"Grandmother's Left Eye"; *Washington
Alternative Poetry Journal*—"My Father Makes a Sales Pitch," "Old
Customs"; *Waterways*—"At the Wailing (Western) Wall," "Mrs. Wei in
Peking."

My grateful thanks to Barbara Goldberg, mover and shaper, for editorial
inspiration during the final production of this book and for splitting the
orange.

About the historical Chinese characters depicted on the cover:

*The ancient character represented the ritual bearing of the Chinese
women, the arms hanging down, and crossed over the body. The head
was not represented. The shoulders, arms, chest, and legs were outlined.
The character, difficult to write because of the perfectly symmetrical
lines, was modified into a more cursive style.*

—Weiger, Dr. L. *Chinese Characters.* Trans. L. Davrout.
2nd ed. New York: Paragon Book Reprint Corp., 1965.

The CAPITAL COLLECTION is a new series by the Word Works which will feature excellence in poetry from authors in the Greater Washington, DC area. The hallmark of this collection is that each book selected will be financially supported by advance book sales and community contributions.

Manuscripts read for the 1989 publication were invited by the Word Works Editorial Board. All inquiries must include a self-addressed stamped envelope.

The following people made contributions to the 1989 Capital Collection title, *Bad Names for Women*:

Mel Belin
Celia Brown
Harriett Destler
Sue Golan
Beth McGrath
Fay Picardi
Helen Rebull
Carole Robinson
Nancy St. Germain

The Word Works gratefully acknowledges these contributors and those who wish to remain anonymous.

for the Goldbergs—
who never call me bad names
my husband Joe; our daughters
Ilana PuYing, Shoshana MeiYing & Rebecca SuYing
and for my father-in-law Isaac

CONTENTS

WOMAN, BY ANY NAME

BAD NAMES

Eve, Helen, Delilah, Clytemnestra, Jezebel, Witch,
Home-wrecker, Housewife, Gold-digger, Mother-in-law, Hag.

The really bad names are women's
names, rock-heavy with centuries of calumny:
whore, slut, nymphomaniac
are names coated with sewer sludge,
debasement that somehow never stuck
to the quick tails of gigolo, wolf,
pimp, and prick—male names that spin out
light, fluttering like slick-winged ducks
above river marshes and tide pools.

In the marshlands, the women crouch, they
crouch and wait. Tidewater's coming in . . .
Soon, they will rise, will fly
with mud-rinsed wings.

I
CHINESE MOTHER

DAYENU

When I die, my children will say
Kaddish for me and that, with pinewood box
and linen shroud, will be enough.

In time, I will say Kaddish
for my parents. It will not be enough.
They believe in Hell's Yellow Emperor,
fret about food, shelter for their ghosts.
The magnification of an alien God's name
would send them into the afterlife, barefoot
ghosts on hard dirt streets, banging
tin cups on red doors. They would drink
bitter tea, lie alongside ghosts with unopened wombs.

So I have promised my mother I will burn
a paper mansion with puppet servants, chests
of paper gold, paper shells of cars.
My brothers will provide oolong
and chicken rice each feast day, the monthly
stipend of Hell money, shells of faith.
These we render to our mother who tied
red thread on our feet and fingers as we slid
from her womb to bind us to life.

We hold this end of the scarlet thread
our parents unravel as they near the Yellow Springs,
feel it tighten as the wind
blowing off the river, lodges dust in our eyes.

12

MOUNTAINS

"San Ko Wan Yow Yat San Ko"
                    —Ancient Chinese Proverb

When we were arrogant, Mother sang
the old rhyme, *Tall Mountain, there's
another mountain taller.*

We told her about Everest.

And she said, *The highest peaks
don't know their own foothills. They long
for wildflowers, birds to nest in trees,
want to hear voices
warmer than the winds.*

THERE ARE NO KUNGFU FIGHTERS IN MY FAMILY TREE

At ten I knew the magic of words like
please and thank you. I learned
their darker power from a girl who pushed
me from the last seat on the school bus,
used words like karate kicks.

"Leh ka ma hai fa kai, leh ka ba hai fun dhung."
Your mother's a whore! Your father a rice bag.

Yielding the seat, I stared out the window
at the muddy waters of the river we crossed
daily to school, where crocodiles sometimes rose
to swallow in one gulp a woman, whole—shoes,
handbag and frantic eyes.

NURSES

My playboy father loved nurses, told me
never to become one. "Take up teaching,"
he said. "Men do not seduce teachers.
Nurses go down easy." He spoke
from experience, not understanding

how handling bedpans and nakedness, being
intimate with wasted organs, failed flesh could
make a woman reckless, want the embrace
of summer bodies before they chill
into brittle and bones.

"He scrubs his teeth with barren words,"
Mother said. "Nurses are people, there's bad
and there's good. Not that many find him
irresistible." "Just the pretty ones,"
he mouthed at me so she wouldn't hear.
"Just the pretty ones."

MY FATHER MAKES A SALES PITCH

Your mother was fourteen when the match
was proposed. Old Devil Kim Kee
and I on bicycles pedaled five miles to "view" her.
Two hours in heat and dust. Alone, I could
have made it in one. Old Devil, what a tortoise,
kept mumbling "right foot down, left foot down,"
you'd think he never rode a bike before!

I should have listened to my mother. "Too thin
to bear sons," she said. I swore I'd shave my head,
become a monk if she refused the match.
Her parents greeted me like a hero. Japanese
soldiers were snatching virgins.

The war was hard for all. I saw pale
English women sweep the streets in bras
and underpants, their shoulders red
with shame and sun and soldiers' eyes.

I smuggled rice during the war, crossed
the river with fifty *kati* sacks on my back
on dark-moon nights. They caught my friend Yung,
chopped off his hands. I was twenty-three then,
strong as a horse, two horses! The strength's gone
from my legs now. Still, my heart has fire.

Your mother hates risk, no gall bladder.
Savings, that's all she cares about. I gave
her presents. She wanted money to save.
You can't do anything with a woman like that.

16

I swear I'm a saint to stay.
If I splash on cologne, she suspects
I'm off to meet a woman. If I come in late, she hunts
for lipstick marks. My mistresses
were just as unreasonable.

I gave up the woman I loved. She could not wait
till you were grown. But I am not bitter.
I live with open heart, open hand. I let grief
run like money through my fingers.

If I were less generous, I'd be rich today.
All those debts I forgave—until my business failed.
That's my problem—a wide open heart.

At fifty, I tried ballooning in Hajai, at fifty-five, water
skiing. I've eaten dogmeat, bearclaw, iguana, even monkeybrain
in Hong Kong. I've never tasted horse, but I would like to
try it. I hear they serve it in Paris, France.

MRS. WEI GOES HOME TO SHENSI

Aiiyah . . . they told me, they told me true.
See Shanghai, Peking, SiAn first, but I
would not listen. Ancestral village, then

the tours. I never dreamt a family
so extended, so devoted.
They trudge for miles, hitch rides

on two horse-power tractors, pony carts,
arrive begrimed with coal-dust
just to see my face. My traveler's checks

vanish like dew on late morning grass,
exchanged for *yuan*, sacks of rice.
"You must stay to dinner

(and breakfast) before your trip home."
My uncle's wife's brother-in-law
says he rises at five to work the commune farm,

at dark returns to hoe his ginger patch.
It brings in *fen* for thread and cloth.
We serve no banquet, salted radish, rice.

Sun-darkened, sinewy, they gulp
tureens of rice, ask about the legendary
Nanyang gold! Cousin Shiao Lin introduces

the fifth son-in-law of my grandmother's
third cousin. And his family. She whispers, "We need
to buy more rice." I forage in my purse,

18

regret I won't see Shanghai. I must leave
before the money for Peking goes. SiAn went
for eighty cousins yesterday.

MRS. WEI IN PEKING

1

All my life I've wanted to see
this Ten Thousand Li Great Wall.
Now I am sixty-five, too old for change

and Communism, the Malaysian Visa Office
permits I visit the land of my ancestors.
Oh, my arthritic knees! This wall was built

for mountain goats! The Emperor's soldiers—
perched on the edge of the world, wanting
to sow rice and children, making do

with mulled wine against snow and ghost voices
wailing in the stones. Poor dead soldiers—
their breaths chill the stone, the summer wind.
I feel it. This Wall is haunted.

2

So this is the Summer Palace! The guide says
this lake was dug by thousands with shovels.
The Dowager Empress was vain: mirrors

line her pavilions! I can't eat
our banquet of her favorite foods. I've tasted
better in Singapore, San Francisco, Taipei.

The guide says she insisted on one
hundred twenty courses for dinner. No wonder
she grew fat. With her bound feet, no exercise.

Did she eat to forget she poisoned her son?
I wonder where in all this splendor
the bathroom is hidden?

3

Now I'm not fussy about latrines.
I pack toilet paper in my purse,
and know well the Honeyman's scents.

But latrines with doors of air,
exposed as a newborn snail. *Aiiyah!*
This is too bare for me. But after all,

the woman in the opposite stall knows
there's nothing new to see. I'll squat
as she does, turn my eyes to the wall.

MRS. WEI IN AMERICA

In the House

Ants bite my heart when I am alone
in your house. Picture windows invite thieves.
Our houses are safer. Padlocked

iron gates, barred windows, broken glass
on wall ledges keep robbers and salesmen
at a respectful distance.

At the Safeway

The food wrapped in such clean paper,
so many colors! The clever shapes of glass
and plastic. I want to take your containers home

to Malaysia, impress my neighbors.
American meat has no smell. The water
tastes strange, even after boiling.
I'll be glad to be home where foods smell right
and I can argue with the butcher, get an extra
ounce by calling him Miser.

On the Road

Everything here is big, especially the roads.
Cars and their drivers are polite.
Back home, eight tigercars would have squeezed

into the space between this car and the next,
their drivers giving you the finger
for tamely waiting in line.

On Governments

Malaysian Government is like the American
price system: take it or leave it.
It's easy enough to leave a dress hanging

on the rack, but a country is not something
you can get up and walk away from. Your Congress
resembles our marketplace: haggling and shouting

until everyone is a little satisfied.
Can we visit a shop where I can talk
the price down? I want to buy a victory.

I need a good fight.

MRS. WEI IS UNHAPPY WITH THE SEXUAL REVOLUTION

Equal pay, yes, of course. Equal sex
I cannot understand. They are throwing away
years and years of women's work.
A hundred thousand nights, perfumed skin,
pale bodies that pleasured the Emperor until
he groaned "Yes," and passed a decree of monogamy.
In the morning, he added a law for concubines.

From the beginning, women have made men
pay for sex—a leg of wild boar, gold
chains, marriage. Now, their daughters give
it away, call it freedom! And the men,
the men are laughing as they go
from bed to bed to bed. A basket of scuttling
crabs let loose while dog bites dog-bone.

MRS. WEI GOES TO THE DOGS

We Chinese have no use for dogs
except as health food to heat
the blood, like vitamin E or rhino horn.

A flock of geese, their wings raised
like shields, snake-heads a stabbing
of spears, make better houseguards.

Cormorants pay for their board with fish.
My cat earns his place. The day I find
mice in my kitchen, out he goes.

Some people claim a mongrel that chooses
their home brings luck. That must be
why I keep feeding this useless mutt.

MRS. WEI DISAGREES WITH RICHARD WILBUR

*"The snow came down last night like moths
Burned on the Moon."*
                              Richard Wilbur

No, no, it's the Lady-in-the-Moon
doing her laundry, though, living alone, what
has she got to wash? I know, she's cutting
her white rabbit's hair.
Sometimes I worry, she must be bored,
so many centuries on the same old moon,
not even a change of furniture. I know
the first hundred years she was glad
to escape that loud-boasting, wine-swilling
hero husband of hers, but immortality
without family or friends is to dine
on snow, like too long immersion in stale
bath water, tedious till painful.
Centuries of nothing except for the astronauts'
visit. Anything is bearable if you know
it is temporary. Tonight I shall offer incense,
tell her there is talk of a moon station.

MRS. WEI WANTS TO BELIEVE THE FIRST AMENDMENT

That letter telling your President
he is wrong, please don't mail it!
I am so afraid for you. Back home, such

forthrightness will drag you to jail,
your family will have to hide their name.
Or worse, a noose on the raintree, only the wind

to keep your ghost company. Speaking out
is like flying a kite, a banner for police
to track you down.

In my country, we have learned
to fly kites under the bed.

KITEFIGHTING SEASON

*The aim of Malaysian kitefighting is to make other flyers lose
their kites by slicing their strings with your kitestring.*

A sardine can over a small flame
between two bricks. Our illicit fire
behind the woodpile hazed and swirled
heat in slow curls broken by tugs of wind.
My brothers and I on our haunches
watched our glue simmer, sprinkled
powdered glass as it cooked.

We pounded more medicine bottles,
pulled string through glass-spiced glue. The boys
had spent days making their rice paper kites,
painted them ferocious red and black,
all teeth and eyes. Now they permitted me,
a girl, to pound glass, feed the fire with twigs,
hang the glass-fanged string to dry.
Allowed to help, I felt proud to fetch
water, wash glass-grit from cut fingers.

Two days later, my brothers ran in fields
forbidden to girls, forbidden to me. Their kites
leaped skyward, laughing into battle.
I watched kites swoop and dance, eager
to slash glass-coated leashes. I kicked
the ashes from our fire, wished
their kites would elope with the wind.

THE MAN

The nuns taught us sins
are snakes that crawl
into our bodies. Sins nestle
in the dark spaces our evils
hollow within us. The priest
has the power to fill holes
with the light of absolution.
Snakes flee from the confession box.

The first time I saw a flasher
in full cobra life, he was
holding onto his sin, eyes
hard and agate as Lucifer's
in the nuns' picture books. I ran.

I shuddered when Mother said,
"*ku-ku-chai* on boys turn
into *thew-peen* on men
to make babies in women."

Hellfire and snakes, sins erased
with Hail Marys in the morning. Flesh
and blood, maturing, recognized
the serpent had its place in Eden.

GRANDMOTHER'S LEFT EYE

Grandmother saw ghosts with her left eye.
All self-centered and rude, she said,
but Lao Pan's spirit was the rudest.

She said dead Lao Pan came often
to count the inventory
when she was night watchman
in his store. He moaned about strange
chairs and beds no one would buy.
His sons wasted his legacy.

She told him to leave her alone,
business was good. "Go start
a furniture store in Hell if
you have nothing better to do."

"The Dead have enough furniture.
Their children burn paper mansions
with servants and cars for them.
You're a stupid woman. I told Chun
when he married his son to you, he'd picked
a stupid girl," dead Lao Pan spit at her.
Real spittle—Grandmother swore
she had to wipe her face dry.

COUSIN LO'S GIFTS

Cousin Lo achieved licensed driver status
when she was fifty-five. Her sessions
left her instructor shaking, hands
greasy from clutching his brilliantined hair.
It took him four years
to get the "Learner" off her plate.
On the way home from the test, she ran
her little black Ford
into the rear of a vegetable truck.

In her fashion, Lo was generous.
She'd rattle up to our house with gifts:
oranges with just a tad of mold, sour
drops melted into a lump, damp tea
leaves you could dry in the sun.

Her best gift: a trunk of shoes, yellow
slingbacks, red taps, alligator courts,
embroidered see-throughs. All size fours.
Mother looked at her own wide feet,
and thanked her politely.

For months we were Hong Kong movie stars:
Lin Dai, Chin Pei Pei. Then Lin Dai
overdosed on sleeping pills, the Press
discovered Chin Pei Pei was alcoholic.
Our feet outgrew Cousin Lo's shoes.

When the styles came back, Lo regretted her gift.
We'd broadened the shoes too much for her.
Thereafter, she gave us stale sponge cake
and built closets for her shoes.

SAN CHI

Three weeks after death, the deceased's spirit must leave the house and begin its journey to the Land of Ghosts. This night is the zenith of the ghost's power: it can commandeer a living relative for a companion on its trip. It is customary to offer substitutes of paper people.

Father saw Grandmother at midnight
on the twenty-first day after her death.
Earlier, Mother had burned a paper man
with parasol to shade Grandmother
from the sun, to carry her packages
of food and money. At nightfall, her spirit
would begin the long journey
through treeless lands to the Yellow Springs.
"I never believed that nonsense," Father
said, "but she was here. I saw her
standing at the door to the living
room. 'Mother, is it you?' I asked."

She wore her shroud suit, grey silk
tunic and black pants she kept folded
in tissue paper for eighteen years.
The creases jutted from her bony frame.
Eyes like a sleepwalker, she looked
at the latest family photograph, touched
her tobacco box, her cane recliner
that creaked softly to her breathing
during her afternoon nap.

Looking at her recliner, Father said, "She was
saying goodbye to her things, but
she wouldn't speak to me." Mother began
to light incense sticks: "Had she spoken,
you would have died. Why do you think
I burned that paper man? Gods, gods,
thank you for protecting my fool."

OLD CUSTOMS

After 40, Chinese women retire
into the sexlessness of old age, somber
in black pants and grey tunics: pale greys
like ash from last night's fire, dark
silks the forbidding sheen of gunmetal.

They claim the privileges of being old, rest
stiff as ancestral tablets on family altars.

They fold their hands in their laps and watch
their husbands vie with sons, trapped
in the pull of flesh and blood.

II
JEWISH MOTHER

EVE

And the man said, ". . . she shall be called Woman, because she was taken out of Man."

Genesis 2.23

In the beginning was
the Morning of the World and Elohim,
we called him El, wearied of word games,
fetched me to help his Boy call names into Being.
"Blintzes," Adam pointed to the green
softness of our sleeping place. "No," said I,
"Moss is better, a greener, sleepier word."

When I took inventory, he had done
the trees, had begun to call the animals.
I knew the ibis, nightingale, whippoorwill,
heard them name themselves in song.
Spider wove hers in dewdropped silk but Adam
walked into it, broke her web.
Scratching his head, he told Dog to stop
sniffing at his blintzes, threw moss at Cat meowing
in the olive tree, teeth a glitter of laughter.
He loved the word "Nymphomaniac." I couldn't
give a bird or flower so heavy a name so
I held it for safekeeping.

Loneliness I knew in the Morning of the World.
El took Adam on trips, doing he-man stuff.

36

Lilith was my secret friend. We thumb-wrestled,
ran races, climbed trees until El stripped her of arms,
legs and voice, stretched and wrung her into a rope
he flung away to slither into the green wheat.
I never liked him—spoiled brat El
who kicked us out of his personal amusement park
because we touched and tasted his Mystery Fruit.
Still chewing, Adam named it: "Apple,
Apple Cider, Apple Sauce, Apple Pie . . . ."

Adam, Adam, I promise I'll find things
for all your names, I'll learn to change
wheat into flour, I'll invent
fire and baking powder.

That was the first time I sprinkled
Golden Rod on his chest and Moonflower
in my hair. After, Adam said, "From this day,
I shall call you Eve, for you are life,
you are joy, you are flesh quickening."

RUTH TAKES A CHANCE

Believing they were the last survivors of Sodom & Gomorrah,
Lot's daughters plied him with wine and begot the people of
Moab from him. Ruth, the great-grandmother of King David
was a Moabite.

Naomi could be wrong. Mothers-
in-law often are. Yet I believe
her advice feeds my need. That Boaz
desires me, I know. I have seen how
he squares his shoulders, sucks in
his stomach at my approach. Despite
my aching back, I've not missed
how his eyes flicker from counting
ripe barley bushels to my sweat-
soaked bodice at the end of day.

She bathed me tonight, fresh water
instead of her used bath water, her mouth
at my ear whispering tricks
to seduce the man. How came she by such
whoremistress's lore?
"Feign restless sleep," she said. "Sigh
and turn, toss a knee across his manhood,
nestle your breasts against his arm, pillow
your cheek there like a bird come home.
No man who eats red meat can resist
such flattery. Nature will ensure it!"

"And after," I asked, wanting surety,
"what follows the night?"
"We hope he is an honorable man," she said,
eyes bright with the gambler's fevered faith
the dice will fall her way.

Easy for her, it's not her body
will feel the stones and bleed
if I am called whore! I could have stayed
like Orpah and married a cousin, in Moab
all men are my cousins, and freakish.

I will have healthy children from Boaz.
How strange, how beautiful he is—
the right number of toes on his feet.

THE DAUGHTER OF SURVIVORS

for Elaine

She is screaming again.
You stand at your bedroom door.
Her dream claws her sleep to shreds.
Shivering, you will her to stop, will it
to go away. Your father's voice
rises and falls with the burden of her name.

She is awake. You hear her voice cling
to his, as a shipwrecked cat
digs its claws into a floating spar.
You hear the creak of bedsprings as they rise.

Soon, the kettle whistles in the kitchen.
When you peer in, they are huddled together
over the kitchen table. Her pale hands clenched
around the teacup, she whispers her dream.
He has heard it six million times,
but he listens, his arm clamped around her
to contain her shudders.
He, too, has bad dreams, different faces,
the same sequence of events.

You are afraid of this trembling woman
who replaces your mother each night.
You want the daylight woman
who bakes honeycake, and brushes your hair
smiling, as if you are her good dream.

Your father does not change at night.
He, too, fears the knock on the door.
He makes you learn street maps
by heart, sends you out alone
on the New York Subway so that
if you should come home from school
and find them missing, you would
know how and where to run.

ELAINE

Elaine when I first knew her
exchanged stories with the wind,
she would bend to hear a bull frog
interrogate the air.
Between then and last, darkness
and rain filled her mouth, her eyes.
She was gone, closed into herself.
I said: Elaine, the morning is here.
The boat leaves soon, the Lady waits.
There was no answer.
Curled softly around her root
in the liquid dark, she did not answer.
I cried: Elaine, the boat goes,
the Lady will not wait.

2

She is not here,
she has gone
down to the place
where sea anemones swell
and weddings are held at half-past three.

She has gone
by hidden ways
only the raindrops know
to wed a groom with tentacles and hooded eyes;
the polyps naked dance sloughing their shells
to deck the bridal bed.

And sometimes a lost wave
cries her name.
She cannot come:
those are fins that were her hands
those are gills mouthing sand.

WOMEN

Down among ants, one
forgets how slow a tree leans
against changing sky.

The silence of eyes
is the silence of old oak
holding ant cities.

Go watch the wild geese
fly past the tethered moon. Write
our names in water.

AT THE WAILING WALL

At the Wall, hands in your pockets
to display indifference, you said:
There are ants in the Wall.
Cities, civilizations of ants
are building mighty ant empires
and shrines in our destroyed Temple.

Caterpillars munch their pilgrimage
through tough wall weeds
to be consecrated into moths
or butterflies. They think
metamorphosis depends
on what they do or eat. They
have not heard of genetic destinies.

You picked a curl of paper
from its niche in the rocks
and read the prayer for a Jewish Santa Claus,
mocking the simple faith of another.
Later, when you thought I was not looking,
you pressed a curl of prayer
into the ancient stone.

BEDS

Orthodox Jews don't buy double beds.
Such beds are unkosher though no pig
or shrimp touches them. A woman is unclean
at her time of the month and the seven days
that follow. Her husband may not drink
from her cup or lie with her until she goes
to a *mikvah* by the light of evening stars
and all contamination is washed away.

This may be why our men have a reputation
as good husbands. I wouldn't take a wife
for granted if I had her only two weeks
out of four, less if she postpones her bath.

DANCING THE HAKAFOT

Once a year, the Writings of Moses, each
a roll of goatskin parchment and ink the weight
of a fifty pound sack of rice, are taken
from the Ark and paraded exuberantly around
our synagogue. Seven times, the Torah Scrolls
are handed with ceremony to a new bearer.
While the Cantor bellows marching melodies, we clap
our hands and circle the bearers. They march,
dance, tentative steps turning into wild leaps
and can-cans, their hands tight about the wood handles.
Sweat runs into their eyes. Skullcaps fly.
The Torah crowns and breastplates jingle.
Children dance with their mothers, wave flags,
laugh at their fathers' acrobatics.

This year, our synagogue allowed women
to dance the HaKafot. Hair streaming from headscarves,
we panted out songs and twirled with the men.
Eager hands reached out to touch the Scrolls
on our shoulders as our daughters ran behind us.

In a corner, the retired rabbi reproves
his wife with harsh words. Infected
with the momentum of the young, she has broken
a lifelong taboo. She has carried the Torah
with bare, female hands. She will never do it
again, she promises, nodding and clapping
as the last procession begins. Her daughters
dance the HaKafot, their eyes know her joy.

SUKKOT WITH LAURA JACOBS

For seven days you shall dwell in huts; every citizen in
Israel shall dwell in huts, so that your generations know that
I made the children of Israel dwell in huts when I brought
them from the land of Egypt—Leviticus 23:33-34

You said when you wake up after Yom Kippur and
the window and walls are bouncing crazily,
you know Jerry is in the trees, buzz-sawing
s'chach to roof the sukkah, that fragile hut
of bamboo and canvas incongruous as a beggar
in a limousine beside your brick mansion.

The children love tying apples and onions,
carrots and plastic grapes to dangle from the s'chach,
think it the height of adventure to snuggle
into their sleeping bags and count the stars
playing peekaboo through the leafy roof.

Six of seven mornings, we wave the palm and willow
and praise the Lord who has given us sustenance.
We pray the Almighty to send us rain water
in its proper seasons, the early rain and the late
but not too much, remembering cattle drowned
in Texas, and Bangladesh boats moored to rooftops,
swollen bellies of starving children.

Taking down the sukkah, dry leaves like rain
from the roof branches, we discard the rotted
peppers, eat the still crisp apples, save
the plastic grapes for next year. Soon, nothing
remains except a square of trampled grass
where we obeyed the commandment and remembered
we are, generations after, still God's
migrant workers.

JAFFA ORANGE I

ALIYAH

There are no orange groves in Jaffa.

It is a place of white stone, staired streets
overlooking Andromeda's Rock and the Mediterranean.
Jaffa is chic with artists' studios and
furriers' display houses. Except for the *shuk*,
market street where Jews in black suits
live and preserve tradition.

"What lovely times we had together,"
writes my mother-in-law,
inviting us to Israel again.
'Lovely' was her word. 'Ordeal' was mine.
Joe called it 'duty.' I remember the nights
we sat and held our plane tickets,
counted the days. His mother
was powerless over time.

The spotlight intensity of a long summer
with new in-laws without respite
will kill a seedling marriage.
Ours could not have endured without
the refuge of Reb Kahan's study.

Joe's mother was beautiful. At fifty,
hair rinsed chestnut, body full-figured
in pink swimsuit, she drew whistles.
Using herself as a model, she lectured me
on health and diet deficiencies.
She would mold me into a good wife,
fit mother for her grandchildren.

Each morning I followed my father-in-law
to the market while Joe endured
his mother's strictures on our doomed
cross-cultural match. Afternoons, she
marched us to the beach, analyzed
my ego on the sand. She found my life goals
unsatisfactory. Joe taught me
to swim, but you can stay in the water
just so long and still have recognizable skin.

"You have married a poor man," she said
that summer. "Only his brain stands
between destitution and your children."
Have a heart, I thought. We'd been married
three months. I was on the pill.
"Don't look to us for an inheritance.
You have to cherish Joe's brilliant mind,
keep it free from distractions, do his
personal letters." Now she complains
he does not write though she loves
my letters and is glad we married.

*

My father-in-law, a mild man with gentle
eyes, accepted me without probation.
I remember our morning excursions
to market as ceasefire interludes, Dad
pointing out people and places of interest.
Everyone knew him, greeted him
with chatty updates on family news.

A man in a second floor window
stirred my interest. Always, he stared
over the street where men and women haggled
in muscular Hebrew over vegetables, stomped
more dirt into the veined cobblestones
worn smooth by generations of sandaled feet.

"That's Reb Elihu Kahan from Vilna,
a notable scholar," my father-in-law said.
"He speaks seven languages."

Reb Kahan and Alfred Hitchcock
could have been brothers. In their sixties,
some common forebear's DNA surfaced, shaped
their bodies, twinned their faces though
Reb Kahan hid in a bushy white beard
and curling sidelocks.

It was plain he and Joe's Dad got high
on talmudic reasoning. I invited myself
to their afternoon sessions where
they became flushed of face
and high-voiced in pursuit of exact
interpretation of *pilpul*.
Moses meekly stood on the frayed rug
while they examined his character like two tailors
tracking seams in his pants.
While Joe went to the beach with his mother,
I'd watch Reb Kahan debate
the fine lines on both hands
of a word, a sentence, the probable
age of Ruth when she followed Naomi.
He traced genealogies for weeks,
let dinners congeal and arrived
at an octogenarian Boaz, Ruth a bride at forty.

50

*

Often, before we knocked, we'd hear him
whistling behind his study door.
He told me he had tried, as a boy, to stop.
Whistling attracted demons. "Pooh pooh pooh,"
his mother, bless her memory, would scold,
flicking salt around him. "You'll bring *shaydim*
into the house." She'd stick a thread in his mouth.
"Chew it," she said as she sewed a hem on his cuff.
"We shouldn't sew up the brains."
He remembered her face, framed by wisps of hair
strayed from the ugly wig she wore daily.
And the smell of *k'nubble*, little bags of garlic
she strung around his neck for health.
Pinches of salt in his pockets: his mother
believed demons breathed down their necks.

His wife, more modern, said she stuck
a safety pin for luck in all his clothes.
He told me she had beautiful hair,
on their wedding day,
how red it had glowed.

Reb Kahan's eyes burned bluer as he hunted
meaning to its lair, tracking its spore
by inferences, connotations, even commas.
His restless cigar scattered ash, missing
containers moved in hopeful circles by Mrs. Kahan.
She baked his favorite *mandelbrodt*,
almond cookies fresh every day.

The only time I heard him speak to her,
he said, "This tea is cold."

JAFFA ORANGE II

PILPUL WITH THE REBBE

Three afternoons a week, I caught a bus
into town, studied for my conversion with
Rebbitzin Seigel. The celebration of Passover,
the proper blessings for Friday nights, on seeing
a rainbow, a crippled child. I learned
rituals, how to pluck a chicken
without the help of boiling water, to singe
its pinfeathers off with a candle, to drain
its blood with coarse salt, to keep meat
and milk from mingling.

"Symbols!" Reb Kahan snorted.
"She teaches you symbols. Change
must be of the mind's heart."

I argued that symbols were necessary, that
the mind's heart, as he called it,
needed time to grow roots.

"You may be right," he said. "But she should
teach you Hebrew, and the Books of Moses."

He grumbled no one listened to him
at the Religious Ministry, spoke
about the relevance of Torah and tradition
in our lives and lent me his commentaries
on the Bible.

Awe and respect had been his daily due
in his old country. Now, he was just one more
rebbe in a land of rabbis, his voice
unheard, his plumage indistinct
as a blackbird's in a sky filled with crows.

52

*

In the dark hall outside the Reb's study,
Mrs. Kahan whispered worries in Yiddish
to my father-in-law. To me, she said,
"He chainsmokes all week—except on Sabbath."

She tugged her kerchief tighter over
her drab brown wig, pushed a stray
brightness of red hair back into concealment.

Dad told me she feared the Reb was depressed.
"*A mentsch tracht und Gott lacht*
he's been saying each night. *A man thinks
and God laughs.*"

I wondered if she pillowed his head
on her breast or hid more luck pins
in his pockets. Or both.

Their daughter, Rachel, married
a man the Reb despised, a modern
Israeli who drove on Saturdays.
Rachel wore a kerchief when she visited
but Reb Kahan knew—his daughter displayed
her red hair like a harlot,
humming as she wove her way through
the city of half-naked women with tanned shoulders,
bared heads, baby carriages.

I asked if my uncovered head bothered him.

He shook his head. "Your conversion—
does sorrow dwell in your parents' house?"

I explained Chinese daughters were expected
to follow their husbands' religions.

"I will tell you a story. Two rebbes
are walking from Beersheba in the morning.
One rebbe goes to Jerusalem. The other
is going to Hebron, which is halfway
to Jerusalem. In Hebron, they are both killed
by a terrorist's bomb. Yet only one is a failure."

I considered his story in silence.

He nodded, said simply, "I am that man
going to Jerusalem. I am the failure."

*

At the close of one Sabbath, he drank
his sweet wine, doused the braided *Havdolah*
candle and went as usual to his room.
Using a clothesline, he leapt off
a flimsy scaffolding of books.

We visited Mrs. Kahan as she sat *shiva*.
"Why?" she cried. "He was a man
who broke new ground in his thinking.
In Vilna the rabbis acclaimed him."
He left no note, no explanation.

Huddled on her mourning stool, she held
an ashtray in her lap, said, "It was just
like him to wait till Sabbath was over."

There are no orange groves in Jaffa.

III
WOMAN, BY ANY NAME

ODALISQUES WERE INVENTED BY MEN

A man loves
the image of his dog waiting
in a lonely house for the sound
of his footstep, his key
in the lock, tail wagging,
eager to chase his stick.

A LIBERATED WOMAN

She had both of them that week.

Tim recalls the roosters, tail feathers
iridescent blue and red, razors
tied to their claws.

Chuck remembers the Silat dancers, men
in panther-black, their bare feet
edging dirt sideways as they circled, tensed,
leaped, kris knives carving silver
spirals in the firelight.

That was the night the men wrestled
tug o' war, her arms their rope.
They laugh now about that episode
with Norani Whats-her-name.

She remembers their full names, wrote them
in orange juice in her little black book.
Being a woman, she knows who crossed
her threshold and who entered.

THE FIRST TIME IS ALWAYS A DISAPPOINTMENT

He promised her passion, promised
he would cover her with roses, he needed
his soul to drown in her hair.

She could not know: a young man's sex
is beyond control, a thing possessed
by the heave and surge of blood; wild

horses in his groin would rear
over her and break away while she,
pumping her legs, is left

behind, without transport
while he rides the untamed and comes
panting back to fall across her breasts

into sleep, hoofbeats fading in his chest.
"Is that it?" she asks, staring at blood
red petals on her thigh.

YOU'VE COME A LONG WAY, BABY

Grandmother said in her time deflowered maidens
threw themselves down the village well
to redeem their family's honor—I detect
some hostility in this suicide/pollution.
A rope was equally handy.

"Defend your virtue like a walled city," she said.
Surrender meant death in the old days.
Widows and married women who yielded
their flesh were tied in pig-baskets
and drowned in the nearest lake or river. The clan
merely broke the lover's legs as a lesson
not to rove among livestock. Today

they write the names of loose women on walls.

BREACH

You told me her name was Leah.
Leah who scoffed at old-fashioned
marriage vows, whispered her room number, how
she slept naked, waiting for a real man.
You paced your hotel room, the hot
Indonesian night pulling wetness from your skin,
counting the steps to her unlocked door.
But you did not go to her, you said, rocking me
in your arms, expecting praise.

The left side of our bed is tilting,
the sheets slide from under us and drop
over the edge. I watch the inner coils
push at the mattress binding, silent upheavals
behind the light and dark of your hip and thigh.

In the street, parked cars climb onto curbs
into bushes. Trees pull away,
drift skyward. A bridge takes its iron
roots out of gravity, rises
and rocks slowly in the air. People
caught in the ordinary act of crossing
catch at the rails. They stare as the river
leaves its bed, water splaying, thinning
into nothing without the containment
of earth and embankments.

SHADOWS

I will tell you what troubles me
when old girlfriends call,
when your secretary details her sex life over lunch.

It is the dog that sleeps by the hearth fire,
neckfur bristling, rising stiff-legged
at the window to eye new shadows in the garden.
You accuse me of confused priorities, how
I remained calm the time you almost died.
Fatalistic Asian, I know dying, being involuntary,
cannot change what is between us.
It is only an absence, a business trip.

But your snake-bite leaving to lie
with another will taint my blood.
My teeth will find sand in my ricebowl.

THE BODY IS WEAK

You say as I crawl into bed
beside you, naked, sun-toasted,
"We don't have to make love." I want to
answer: My soul is pouncing
on your soul's gift, biting
the Eau Sauvage cologne at your neck,
the line of your jaw just shaved for me.
But I am too tired and my mouth's asleep.

THE DEATH OF FISH

In our house, the death of fish is no longer
a calamity. The children have learned death is not
unbearable, have moved from their first
wild refusal of loss. They shape grief
with rituals: they choose a proper grave
in the garden, a fitting rock,
parting words for beloved hamsters
Peanut, Snowball. Echo the guinea pig
lies beside Goliath, the largest four-year-old
goldfish in the world. Each death has been
an inoculation. This morning, Rebecca found
a triangle of wood, a nice marker,
she said, for when Shoshana's hamster dies.

MAMA WASHINGTON ON HOW TO FRY FISH

Girl, when you fry fish, you keep your eyes sharp set
and your stick handy for them alley cats, they don't care
nothing for the hole behind your ribs, faster than you can say
Scat! they're gone and your dinner too. And speak of Toms,
you know that boy's gonna leave soon's he done sowing,
soon's he done plowing your field. You know time for
the harvest, he'd be gone like yesterday's dinner, like old
Tomcat when the moon stomach's fit to burst. My mama, she say
the same thing to me. "Girl," she says, "don't give your body
with your heart." Only us women, we be real fools.

MAMA WASHINGTON'S DAUGHTER TALKS BACK

Easy for you to talk. Find a man
with a heavy pay packet and he'd treat you
good, like an equal! You've got more
rights than any woman wants
here at the bottom where you've got
to count the pennies and power lies
in muscles and Mama, you got no time
for arguing whose turn it's to lug
out the garbage when the children's
crying and pulling on your skirt
and you've got to haul out
that bucket and brush, get on your knees
and scrub for bucks, never mind jam
or chittlings while your man
is hushing the kids, it's his turn
to sleep and dream of leaving you, welfare
paying better than your jobs.

Easy for you to say: Don't go
with losers. You marry
the people you meet and who am I
gonna meet living on our street,
selling makeup at Hecht's?

MAY MEANS BEAUTIFUL IN CHINESE

We name daughters
Yee May, Soo May, Yin May, May May
May Wan, May Choo, May Li, as if
Beauty is the main imperative
for a woman, as if the naming
will make it fact. We load a diversity
of hopes on sons: Ying for courage,
Ming for brilliance, Fook for fortune,
Tai for greatness, and for honor
and endurance, Chong Yan.

Only when bad luck demons pester
a son with sickness and accidents do
we hide his maleness, call him Cat
or Dog. Ah Mow and Ah Gow are common
lifesaving names. If this ploy fails,
there's one sure way to turn away a demon:
disguise your son's value behind a girl's
name, call him Beautiful.

THE NAMING

It all began with Mother,
Mother who called me *nui*,
word meaning female, meaning daughter,
gave me a doll to cherish, made me
addicted to tidiness, driven to fulfill
each commitment. She spoke of an imperfect world
and women its caretakers, how bulls were
like men, responsive to the gentle
tug of a nose ring, they run
from sticks and hard voices.

My husband Joe names me Wife, meaning
lover, caretaker, mother of children,
keeper of his faith and lineage, gives me
the lamp to light his way home.

Now my daughters name me, believe
I am everything, ring me with needs.
In their faces, I see the past
and future, time rippling curves of faces:
grandfather's, mother's, Isaac's, Joe's, they rise
and vanish like the wind's breath on water.
I accept their naming. I am kin
to Poet Chu Yuan's self-drowned body
nibbled to nothing by river fishes.

LINT FILTER

Monday is not her wash day. Tuesday is.
Monday she bends and gathers the weekend
blooms—toys, clothes, the children
think the hamper is to sit upon.
The rug has sprouted newspapers, crumbs,
socks with irreconcilable differences.
As she bends and bends, pain unfurls pink
mimosa nettles in her back.
As she ricochets, an endless pendulum,
she begins again to create
order out of chaos. Tomorrow she will
separate light from dark.

SALT AND THE SWORD

On Ku San Mountain, a clan of warrior women
practiced a unique contraception: salt-free
diets for young men they captured for amusement.

After years of service and bland food, wasted men
came down the mountain cursing and striking
at village women, brooding on vengeance, impotence.

Their prayers were answered when Jia Jen came.
After a hearty breakfast of salted radish, he
went hunting on Ku San Mountain and was taken

behind the stone walls. In captivity he performed
heroically, secretly drank his own urine.
Word of heavily pregnant warriors brought

the Emperor's army, a typhoon that leveled
walls, plowed braided hair and foetal bones
into the ground to add Ku San to Empire.

On the mountain, tall yarrow ripens unpicked.
Catalpa and cassia bloom wild. Birds feed
on mulberries and spider webs glisten everywhere.

In the old gardens, a monkey sampling a peach
pauses, disturbed by a memory and a smell
of salted radish on the evening wind.

GLOSSARY

Aliyah	Literally ascent, going up: the honor of being called up to the Torah in the synagogue. Also used in other contexts, e.g., emigration to Israel.
Blintzes	Thin pancake rolls filled with fruit or cheese.
Chu Yuan	Fourth-century Chinese poet who drowned himself after sending a letter to the Emperor urging less self-indulgence and greater concern for the people's welfare. The Dragonboat Festival commemorates his deed. The Chinese drop dumplings wrapped in bamboo leaves in the river so the fish will not eat Chu Yuan's body.
Dayenu	"It is enough for us": song sung at Passover praising God for freeing the Hebrews from slavery in Egypt.
Elohim	A name of God in Genesis.
Fen	Unit of Chinese money: four fen equal one cent.
HaKafot	Processions in the synagogue during Sukkot, especially on Simhat Torah when the annual cycle of Torah readings is completed and begun over again.
Havdollah	The ceremony for the departure of the Sabbath.
Kaddish	This sanctification prayer praising God is recited by the bereaved daily for eleven months and on the anniversary of death.
Kati	Malaysian unit of weight: one kati equals one and a third pounds.
Kris	Malay long dagger with wavy blade.
Li	A Chinese mile.
Lilith	Female demon: origin linked to Babylonian snake-goddess. According to one legend, Lilith was Adam's first wife and Eve was created after Lilith had left Adam and refused to return.
Mikvah	Jewish bathhouse for ritual purification.
Moabite	Descendant of the union of Lot and his daughters. Believing they were the sole survivors of the destruction of Sodom and Gomorrah, they plied their father

with wine and seduced him to begin the human race again. The Bible mentions giants with six toes, etc. The Philistine giant, Goliath, is believed to be the descendant of Orpah, Ruth's sister-in-law.

Moon Goddess Shang-O, the moon goddess stole, from her husband Yi the Archer, the immortality pill (his reward for shooting the world's excess suns). She flew to the moon and lives there with a white rabbit and a celestial toad.

Pilpul A scholastic form of analysis and debate used in talmudic study.

Rebbitzin A rabbi's wife.

S'chach The leafy branches that form the roof of the succah.

Shaydim Yiddish: demons.

Shiva, shivah The seven days of full mourning immediately following burial.

Silat Malaysian: a stylized martial arts dance.

Sukkah A temporary hut or booth used during Sukkot.

Sukkot, Succoth A major Jewish festival, recalling the harvest festival of thanksgiving and commemorating God's protection during the forty years' journey in the wilderness.

Torah The Pentateuch: the first five books of the Old Testament written by Moses.

Yellow Emperor, Yen-lo The chief king of the Chinese Underworld, the lord over fourteen hells, some say eighteen.

Yellow Springs The river the dead must cross to get to the Chinese Underworld.

Yuan Chinese unit of money: four yuan equal one dollar.

ABOUT THE AUTHOR:

Hilary Tham was born in 1946 in Kelang, Malaysia. She is a graduate of the University of Malaya and a Jenny Moore Fellow. She has been tutor to Malaysian princesses, health insurance claims reviewer, chairman of the coalition to resettle Vietnamese refugees in Northern Virginia, and is president of her synagogue sisterhood. She lives in Arlington, Virginia with her husband and three daughters and teaches creative writing in high schools. Her poems have been published in Malaysia, Singapore, England, Israel, and the United States. Her work is included in *The Second Tongue*, a definitive anthology of Malaysian poetry. Her previous books are: *No Gods Today* and *Paper Boats*. *Bad Names for Women* won second prize in the 1988 Virginia Poetry Prize.

ABOUT THE ARTIST:

A member of The Washington Calligraphers Guild and the Society of Scribes, Robert J. Groner has been certified as a scribe by the Union of American Hebrew Congregations. Mr. Groner earned a master's degree in Asian Studies from the University of Michigan. His work is displayed in private collections, public buildings, and elsewhere. He has been commissioned by a White House conference, businesses, and others.

by Michael Hauptschein